GO!

Career Change Solutions

Dr. M. Jordan

Dedication

This book is dedicated to all of the frustrated, wounded, or disillusioned workers who are looking for some hope and encouragement.

TABLE OF CONTENTS

Introduction

Many people find themselves seeking a career change at some point in their life. The fear and uncertainty of changing a career can be overwhelming for many reasons.

Some people seek to change their career because they want to fulfil their true-life purpose. They've simply "had it" with the daily drudge or greed-to-succeed mentality. Many of these individuals are over 40 and pursuing meaningful new directions and goals for their personal and professional life. These workers frequently want to change careers in order to leave their mark on the world or even change the world!

Work life balance is also a factor for many workers who seek to change careers. Proper work life balance is important for maintaining healthy relationships and sound mental health. After all, ask yourself the question: Who will be with me when I die - my family and friends or my boss and co-workers? What really matters in the end?

Unfortunately, many people need to change careers because they have experienced a sudden or unexpected circumstance such as job loss or a physically limiting health related issue. These individuals may have been feeling "comfortable" in their previous employment but now face uncertainty regarding their employment future.

Still, there are others whose work environment is so toxic they have become physically and possibly emotionally ill. For these individuals a career change is both urgent and necessary.

Whatever your reason for wanting to change your career, this book will provide meaningful and practical information to help guide you through the process.

CHAPTER I: LIFE PURPOSE

Finding our life purpose is one of the biggest challenges we will ever face.

Think of a single 24-hour day. If we sleep for 8 hours and work 9 hours, that leaves approximately 7 hours to do everything else! Isn't it critical to consider the quality those useable 7 hours? I don't know about you, but I want my life to have meaning and purpose.

Keep in mind that finding our life purpose should precede career change if possible. Like entering a new relationship too soon after a break-up, we should exercise caution to avoid making the same mistake in our new career. The means that we must think deeply about what we really want to achieve and what is important to us before we make a career change.

Many people have a deep desire to make a career change. They also have a desire to pursue their life purpose but desire alone is not enough to make it happen. On the other hand, desire is a seed that when properly nurtured, generates hope. Hope leads to action. Action leads to CAREER CHANGE.

Hope – Action – Career Change!

How do we actually find our life purpose for career change? Hire a life coach, buy a book, and change jobs until we are fired from all but one like some crazy process of elimination?

Think about things you have done in life that gave you a sense of fulfilment and enjoyment. Did you feel at peace with yourself when you were doing these things?

Maybe you are just beginning to question whether or not changing careers is right for you. In fact, maybe you are not completely sure if you are really happy or not in your current situation.

It's possible to be unhappy and not realize it. I know this sounds silly but think about it carefully. Are you "tricking" yourself into believing that you are happy? Maybe you are simply comfortable in your current situation. Feeling comfortable in a predictable environment or routine is not the same as living a happy and fulfilled life. Just ask your next-door neighbour who is facing a "mid-life crisis"!

Like a mid-life crisis, a career crisis usually happens when we have a sudden awakening that something is completely out of sync with our life. Remember that a crisis is usually not a "good thing" because it often results in wrong decisions or actions that can have long-lasting and quite regrettable implications. For this reason, it's advantageous for us to meditate on our life purpose from time to time so we are not caught off guard as a result of our own complacency.

Using Our Internal Compass to Find Life Purpose

Career change may be our ultimate goal but we need something to guide us through the process so we know we are making good decisions. We can find life purpose through the logical process of learning to read our personal "internal compass". It's easy to sense when we are off course because there is an underlying feeling that something isn't quite right in one or more aspect of our life. True north on our internal compass is located where inner peace, spiritual balance, and a sense of physical well being all come together in proper alignment.

In short, as we improve our ability to read our internal compass we are more likely to accurately to stay on course. Reading the internal compass then becomes a logical exercise in ruling-in or ruling-out whether or not various situations and/or opportunities help or hinder our pursuit of inner peace.

Another way to think of this internal compass is that it is much like a key. The unique grooves in a key are required to unlock the contents of something valuable. Like the diversity of a human fingerprint, each person's internal compass or life purpose "key" is unique. No two people are exactly the same. For this reason, it's important to evaluate your life purpose by your own standards and values. You may respect or envy someone's life purpose but keep in mind that you are unique. No matter how hard you might try, you cannot duplicate their life purpose. On the other hand, it is important to consider lessons learned by others who have forged through the challenges of finding their life purpose.

Be careful when you ask others to help you determine your life purpose! There is always potential for bias, jealousy, or ignorance. *Your* destiny may be well beyond the expectations of others so be a good listener, but form your own opinion. On the other hand, if you hear a trend or a recurring theme in their feedback you might want to pay special attention to opportunities in that area.

Reading Our Internal Compass: Rule-in/Rule-out

Once we choose to let our internal compass help guide us through the decision-making process of major decisions such as a career change and life purpose, we are taking the first step toward job satisfaction.

When we read our internal compass we must do some or all of the following:

(1) Gather information and conduct research. When we begin the process of making decisions according to our internal compass we need to provide our brain with sufficient information. The information-gathering phase of our preparation can be exciting and frustrating depending on how much patience we have. Sometimes the information gathering is very time-consuming.

For example, if we want to change careers from the field of education to the medical field, we might need to gather information about potential job openings in our area. Then, we would look at the skills required to fill these job openings. If we have transitional skills it may be easier to change careers without additional training or instruction.

In addition to gathering information it is often important to conduct our own informal research. Informal research might include a specific inquiry of the salary range for potential positions in our target career within our geographical location.

(2) Ask questions. We are more likely to make good decisions if we are not afraid to ask questions. Asking questions can be difficult if when we don't like the answers. Still, it's important not to allow discouragement to become part of the decision-making process.

If we don't ask the hard questions on the front-end of our decision-making process, we will surly deal with the results of those questions on the back-end. In short, we never want to fool ourselves into "force-fit". Forcing the fit usually has negative consequences after the illusion of happiness wears off.

(3) Determine if the ROI (return on our investment) is "worth it". For example, if our skill set does not match the skills required for our target career, we may need additional instruction. If the instruction requires the acquisition of a degree, do we have the time and money to invest? If so, will the salary be sufficient to justify the expense? If the answer is yes, what university offers the best value in a quality education? (This question requires us to conduct a bit more research.)

Relocation is another example of a major decision that requires some serious deliberation. Before taking a new position, ask questions, gather information, and do research. Research the cost of living in the new town. Is the potential salary sufficient to cover the cost of living? Determine moving costs in terms of time, stress, and money.

(4) Evaluate the information against our goals and tolerance levels. Forget emotions on this one and think logically! Do the facts indicate that this potential decision aligns within my tolerance range of what I perceive as acceptable according to my life purpose? Do the facts indicate this decision will align with my goals for work-life balance? Do I anticipate feeling a sense of inner peace? Will this decision enhance or hinder my physical and/or emotional health?

(5) Evaluate the overall timing of events. Is everything falling into place without unusual manipulation on my part? What is happening

around me that seem to fit with the timing of this action? Again, never force the fit; timing is everything!

(6) Compare the information logically against our feelings and emotions. Be ready to accept the fact that this thing you want may not be right for you at this moment in time. Be truthful with yourself no matter how painful it might be. If something isn't in proper alignment with your internal compass you may have regrets later on.

In addition, you may find that you followed all the steps and aligned your inner compass to make the best decision but in the end, it didn't happen. Don't give up! Remember, you only have access to your own internal compass; you do not have all the information. You don't know what information or events are happening on the other side of a decision. Be willing to accept all results, good or bad, as favours. This will help you brush off defeat and move on to your next challenge.

(7) Make a decision to take action or hold steady. If your internal compass aligns and it seems that you are going to be able to take action for change, make sure you have not overlooked anything. If everything checks out, go for it. If you have any reservations (that gut feeling something isn't quite right), hold steady. On the other hand, make sure fear isn't holding you hostage from achieving your success. Action does involve some degree of risk. If you have logically analyzed the situation, you have minimized risk to the best of your ability.

CHAPTER 2: JOB SATISFACTION

Toxic Work Environments

Let's face it; toxic work environments are often the end result of competition and greed. Companies are faced with many difficult challenges within what has become a highly competitive global economy. Most businesses seek to establish those competitive advantages that will endure over time. Since nearly everything can be imitated, it is essential for businesses to be out in front of the competition as the first, the best, and as the original, with the original being better than the imitation. What every business has that its competitor does not is the unique intellectual capital of its employees.

Toxic work environments often result from management paranoia (real or imagined). This happens because employees are both the source and keepers of information that is critical to the competitive advantage of the company; they have an intimate functional knowledge. Thus, managing secrecy becomes an important component of competitive advantage as well because important information that is leaked to a competitor may threaten the stronghold.

Breaches in secrecy may compromise a company's competitive advantage when employees leave their company to work for a competitor; or through deviant behaviors such as sabotage and revenge. Unfortunately, the result of leaks, breaches, sabotage, and revenge contribute to the formation of toxic work environments.

Toxic work environments are dysfunctional and negatively impact us physically and emotionally. If you are currently in a toxic work environment, it is in your best interest to seriously consider a change of jobs or a complete career change.

Toxic work environments often evolve over time in subtle increments. A few indicators of this evolution include increased workloads while management seems insensitive to workers' being overtired and overwhelmed, increased intolerance of employee requests for time off, administrative bullying of workers, increased secrecy and hoarding of information and/or power, and threats to job security for non-compliance of company rules. No wonder workplace stress costs our nation more than $3000 billion each year.

The Continuum of Decision

It has been said, "people change bosses rather than jobs". While this may be true, there are other reasons.

Each person falls somewhere on the continuum of need to maintain their employment in a dysfunctional environment or make a change. Often leaving is the only clear option to maintain one's sanity and health. On the other hand, some people are better able to take action to disassociate themselves from the grip of psychopathic bosses. There are several contributors that impact one's decision to stay or leave their dysfunctional environment:

• Perceived need to overcome the situation rather than be branded "a quitter".

• Fear of leaving the known to pursue the unknown. Many people prefer to remain in a dysfunctional environment than venture into the unknown of working for another company.

• Belief that if they work harder the boss will eventually become pleased with their performance; or, that everything will eventually improve.

• Disbelief. They fail to trust their own observations; they may even form a mental block against belief that what is happening is real.

• Self-esteem. For some individuals, their self-esteem is directly connected to the company for whom they work. Much of their life may have been given to the company; therefore, to leave would be especially traumatic.

• Health benefits. Some people feel they are unable to leave because the health benefits are assisting with their medical needs or the needs of family members.

• Salary. Many people are not in a financial position to risk being unemployed for an unknown period of time. Financial fears are powerful drivers in one's decision to stay or leave their environment.

• Power, wealth, and greed. Some people have a belief that if they closely align themselves to the beliefs and actions of the psychopathic boss they will be in line for promotion, an increase in pay, and additional authority over others.

It is important to know when we need to change directions, which may include career change. If we are not satisfied with our job or our job does not fulfil our life purpose, we should develop a plan for change. Job satisfaction is an individual decision; it is often determined by our personal tolerance of workplace dysfunction.

Having grown up in the Midwest I watched cows walk to the barn and back day after day in single file. Even though they have the entire pasture at their disposal, they always seem to take the same grass-worn path to their destination.

The following bovine analogy makes a strong point and may be useful in helping you analyze your *own* workplace dysfunction:

HOW THE LEAD MOO COW RUINED HIS VERTEBRAE

Don't think. Don't speak.

Just follow me, for I am the lead moo-cow as you can see.

Just stay on the path; I don't want you to be

A wandering cow. Get back behind me.

So the cows all followed in a line tight and straight.

When the lead cow stopped 'twas entirely too late.

Each cow kissed the ass of the cow by his nose,

But that was just fine, for the line they did close.

The cow in the back moo'd, "Do it again!"

The lead cow moo'd, "Say when!

What fun! What fun! We're such a great team!"

(A long line of ass-kissers is a lead cows dream.)

So the joy and pleasure of taking no risks

Had a long-term impact on the lead cow's discs.

"Don't challenge the system - just get back in line!

Do it my way then things will be fine."

Some of the cows merely want to be free; they think and they speak,

But it cannot be.

"It's Hamburger Highway for you!" they insist.

In dysfunctional systems truth cannot exist.

It should be noted that in dysfunctional work environments, the person who sees and speaks the problem *becomes* the problem. It is always easier for management to remove the problem-seer than resolve the actual problem. Conversely, the health of a company and condition of the work culture is exemplified by the degree of honesty displayed through the communication among and between employees and managers.

Question: Is there a free exchange of truth and a sense of justice in your workplace? If not, *to what degree* is truth allowed?

If there is little truth and justice in your current place of employment, it is probably a toxic work environment! Get ready to GO!

Job-Related Stress

The National Institute for Occupational safety and Health (NIOSH), a division of the U.S. Department of Health and Human Services, is the key agency responsible for research and recommendations pertaining to the prevention of work-related illness and injury. NIOSH is directed by Congress research and analyze workplace stress.

NIOSH has established a model of job stress that describes the relationship between an employee's work and personal life, support networks of friends and colleagues, and the impact of a positive attitude. Given this model as a premise for understanding, NIOSH identified conditions within the workplace may lead to stress:

The Design of Tasks: Heavy workload, infrequent rest breaks, long work hours and shift work; hectic and routine tasks that have little inherent meaning, do not utilize workers' skills, and provide little sense of control.

Management Style: Lack of participation by workers in decision-making, poor communication in the organization, lack of family-friendly policies.

Interpersonal Relationships: Poor social environment and lack of support or help from co-workers and supervisors.

Work Roles: Conflicting or uncertain job expectations, too much responsibility, too many "hats to wear."

Career Concerns: Job insecurity and lack of opportunity for growth, advancement or promotion; rapid changes for which workers are unprepared.

Environmental Conditions: Unpleasant or dangerous physical conditions such as crowding, noise, air pollution, or ergonomic problems.

Achieving Financial Goals

What are your financial goals? Do you need money now or do you have time for a more cautious approach to making a career change?

Our needs and wants often drive our financial goals but this can be tricky as our needs and wants change over the course of our lifetime.

Someone who is unemployed has an immediate financial goal of making money. Yet someone whose family, marriage, or relationship is falling apart due to work-related issues may find their financial goals secondary to their need for work-life balance. Regardless of the reason for career change, our unique financial goals should be given careful consideration.

Maybe we just want to earn more money! Our financial goal may be to retire with enough money to live comfortably and modestly.

For some, financial freedom may a catalyst for career change. We may seek financial freedom as a way to achieve our life purpose. We are positioning yourself for change.

For others, career change isn't about the money at all. For these folks, financial goals are low on the list of priorities compared to priorities relating to life purpose, work-life balance, and job satisfaction.

One day my good friend shared with me that her secret desire for employment is to assign names to new colors of crayons. Even though this is probably not a real employment option, she was expressing a desire to use her creative imagination regardless of the income it would generate. Secret desires like this one cut to the very core of who we are as unique individuals. Often it is our secret desires that hold clear truths about our own strengths and talents.

The Desire to Make a Difference

Do you want to do something meaningful with your skills and abilities? There are lots of ways to make a difference in our world but to do so you have to find the job openings.

Take a look at the job openings on some of the following websites of interest to you. Determine if your skillset is sufficient to bridge to the employers needs or if you need to boost your marketability by additional training and education.

The Ornithological Societies of North America has a job board with positions pertaining to the study and protection of birds. Similarly, the National Wildlife Federation is a wonderful organization the focuses on wildlife. If you care deeply for our nation's wildlife, their website is worth investigating. Another excellent organization for conservation is the Society for Conservation Biology.

One organization that is a particular favorite of mine is the Association of Zoos and Aquariums. This organization is highly respected and the members are held rigorous standards of excellence in the care of captive living creatures. Jobs posted are interesting and often specialized but your skills may be just what they need.

Maybe you want to make a difference, but you want to work where it's sunny and warm. If so, you should be searching for jobs by location. Or maybe you prefer to telecommute (meaning that you work from your computer). A web search for nonprofit and philanthropy and telecommuting & part-time jobs may be a good place to start.

CHAPTER 3: TAKE ACTION

A collection of professional skills and talents is known as a skillset. The skillset is often listed at the top of a resume so prospective employers can use is as a quick way to identify key words applicable to the opening they wish to fill.

Your skillset is by no means everything you know how to do, but does include your most important or most relevant skills. It is important to note that you may have a skillset of five to fifteen skills. Depending on the skills required for the position you wish to secure, you might only list the most relevant on the resume you send to that prospective employer. The key is to put your most relevant skills in front of the person reviewing resumes. Often, the person reviewing resumes only knows enough about the open position to match what the employer is seeking with what prospective employees have to offer.

More specific information on how to use your skillset as a career change bridge is addressed in Chapter 6.

Do your homework before sending a resume. This will save time and make your job search more efficient.

How to Determine Skills Needed

Go to the job posting for a position you are interested in. Look at the skills and education requirements. Compare your skills and education to those needed.

For example – If you are an RN who wants and needs more time off you might go to the local school district's website and search for employment openings as a school nurse. Your basic skill set would be the same, but you have probably never worked for a school district. The recruiter for the school district will want to know if you have the essential skill set but expect to discuss how your skills will transfer to a school environment.

If changing careers is not an urgent matter then you have more time to consider what it is that you really want to do. Think about your skill set then determine what you have to offer a prospective employer.

Maybe you want to work for an environmental organization but all of your work experience is in training or customer service.

That's okay! Search the employment listings of organizations that match your interest and some or all of your previous work experiences.

Using a Functional Resume for Career Change

A functional resume is perfect for those wishing to make a career change. Functional resumes are resumes that describe what you have done in real and concise terms.

Before you begin writing your functional resume, identify your skill set. After that, it will be time to prepare to write your functional resume. You must create your timeline of previous employment, list your education and training history, assemble the 3-5 references willing and able to provide favorable information regarding your skills and personality.

Evaluating Prospective Employers

Job seekers are frequently anxious to secure a face-to-face interview and ultimately a job offer. Haste and anxiousness may result in an unpleasant or even horrible work experience. Consequently, it is best to prepare oneself to enter the interviewing phase of job seeking as a two-sided event. Employers typically view the interview process as tilted to their advantage and preference. Therefore, it is the responsibility of the job candidate to assert the components of an interview that allows the candidate to develop a true and accurate snapshot of the company as a place for potential employment.

Interview questions are one way assess the suitability of the company and, more specifically, the supervisor as a "right fit" for an individual's needs, preferences, and expectations. Samplings of questions to ask a potential employer are:

• What characteristics does the individual who will fill this position need to possess? (Listen for a specific description of characteristics. If the response is vague it may indicate that the manager simply wishes to fill the position rather than match the individual to the job responsibilities.)

• What are the major benefits of filling this position? (Listen for the manager to describe optimism and positive comments regarding the position. Comments should indicate that the manager is deeply familiar with the job responsibilities and supportive of employees.)

• What are the most pressing challenges to be faced in this position? (Honest communication combined with optimism should prevail in this response.)

• How is information shared with employees? (The response should provide some indication that there are regular meetings, training, memo, etc. A better response would include information regarding re-occurring meetings such as weekly, monthly, etc.)

• What are the appropriate channels of communication necessary for employees who have concerns? (The response should be specific as to the procedure for following chain of command and company policy.)

• What types of training or continuing education do employees receive? (The response should indicate periodic formal and informal training. Some companies provide assistance to employees who wish to further their education.)

• Would you describe your view of an ideal employee? (The response should describe general and reasonable expectations. Excessive use of phrases such as "whatever it takes" or "until the job is done" may indicate that the employee will be working long hours.)

• How frequently would I expect to receive feedback regarding my job performance? (The response should be specific regarding formal performance reviews. In addition, there should be some indication of on-going informal feedback.)

• Could you briefly describe the climate of the department? (This response should indicate that the manager is aware of the climate within the department. Beyond awareness, the climate should be described in a positive manner.)

Keep in mind; questions asked by the job candidate make take the employer by surprise, making for an uncomfortable situation. In the event that this should occur, the candidate would be wise to carefully select only the most important questions. In addition, interviews may go beyond the prescribed time allotment if the candidate asks many detailed questions.

As the candidate proceeds through the interview process it is important to be aware of additional indicators of the company climate, communication, and infrastructure. For example, the candidate may wish to consider the following questions:

• Does the interviewer ask the candidate superficial questions that are void of any focus on personal character? There should be some indication that character is a valued aspect of each employee.

• Do all of the interviewers appear to have the same general understanding of company climate? When company communication is adequate, multiple employees are more likely to be able to articulate the same information in various forums.

• Does the interviewer offer the candidate water or the opportunity to use the restroom if the candidate has travelled some distance? Basic consideration of the candidate's well-being should be demonstrated; providing a glass of water or directing the candidate to a drinking fountain should in no way appear to be an inconvenience.

• Does the interview process appear to be decisive and orderly? Does the company contact the candidate within stated timeframes and formats? If the candidate is told that he/she will be contacted by email on a specific day, does this happen? Or, is the candidate contacted two weeks later? Everyone has a busy schedule so some tolerance should be afforded. However, if there is a pattern of grossly delayed communication or no communication this may be a cause for some concern.

Immediate Steps to take if Your Boss is a Psychopath (...and they're out there)

One unfortunate catalyst for career change action is the urgent need to escape a psychopathic boss. If you are currently working for a psychopath you already know it, but you may not know what career change action to take. Forget about your salary because no amount of money is adequate compensation for the abuse you are experiencing. Begin your plan of action for career change today.

Suggested actions for those who find themselves working for a psychopath:

• Update your resume.

• Update your list of professional certifications, training, presentations, projects, and relevant accomplishments.

• Gather current letters of recommendation for your professional file.

• Begin looking for another job (internal or external).

• Begin saving your money. Stop all unnecessary spending until you have a cushion equivalent to a three or four month salary.

• Keep meticulous documentation in an off-site location. Do not share with others that you are keeping documentation or the location of the documentation.

• Assume that email and phone communication is being monitored; refrain from any statements that could be perceived as negative. Do not make comments expressing discontent with the executive or the company.

• Pay close attention to the stated expectations. If necessary, seek clarification of stated expectations and any unstated expectations. Use respectful statements such as, "Is there anything else you would like me to do that I am not already doing?"

• Be respectful of both the person and the position; psychopaths are ego-driven.

• Avoid provoking the executive or engaging him/her in deep dialogue. If not, you will walk away from the discussion with a list of 50 new things on your "to-do" list above your regular responsibilities.

• Avoid arguing.

• Be cautious when "pushing back" even if you are invited to do so.

• Avoid engaging in dialogue with others about the executive in or out of the office. If possible, find a friend to confide in who lives in another city or state and who is in no way connected to the situation or other employees within the company.

• Realize that nothing you do will be sufficient to satisfy this person. If you work 60 hours, the expectation will be that you should have worked 65 hours and taken no lunch break. If you work through lunch and into the evening, the expectation will be that you should have been working on the weekends. If you turn in your project by the deadline, you may be perceived as failing to do your best work. On the other hand, if you miss the project deadline, then you are perceived as unable to manage your time.

• Assume that no one can be trusted completely as a confidant in a stressful environment. Even individuals who have previously kept confidences may be unable to do so under the pressure of the situation. Everyone will be taking care to protect their own livelihood.

• Expect fallout as a result of the ever-changing expectations. People may begin to rally their efforts in an attempt to combat the chaos.

• Expect friends and colleagues to be suddenly terminated.

• Expect complete upheaval within the company or the department when policies or procedures are ignored.

• Expect rapid changes to occur in any and all areas of your work.

• Expect sudden changes in performance expectations to occur. This is especially true if individuals are being terminated because job responsibilities will require adjustment.

• Expect to experience physical symptoms of the stress you are encountering; take care to minimize the symptoms if possible.

• Know your rights as an employee, but beware; unethical and dishonest tactics will be used to discredit you.

• Be prepared to face immediate termination for articulating disapproval with the management of the psychopath.

• If you elect to share your documentation, expect eminent, if not immediate, termination.

• Do not assume that those who work with you share your perspective or will be willing to share any documentation that may protect your employment. Expect to be terminated.

• Remember that if you are doing your best professional work, the problem is not you. Therefore, do not allow the negative comments or dysfunctional environment crush your spirit or destroy your career. Stay focused. Maintain your highest standard of professionalism and performance at all times. Continue looking for another position.

• Do not share with anyone in the office that you are looking for another position. Without exception, this information will travel rapidly to the ears of the executive.

• Avoid taking any time off from the job. Save your time away for interviews with potential employers.

• Expect to see colleagues who are unable to tolerate the pressure of the work environment. Be empathetic and positive. Make statements such as, "I understand what you are feeling. Don't let the stress get to you. You might need to do whatever you have to do to stay healthy and focused until you feel better about things." Such statements acknowledge the problem but do not exacerbate the person's stress level.

• Remain alert. Have a plan of escape should the workplace stress rise to dangerous levels. If you suspect that another employee may become violent take care to stay clear of this employee. Be aware that reporting your suspicions may lead to additional problems for you. Consequently, you must weigh your suspicions against all potential costs incurred from reporting this to your supervisor. Reporting such concerns is tricky because you may not be believed. Instead, you may be perceived as being overly concerned resulting in no action or interest in your observations.

Over 50!

Career change for those over 50 is often very different because competition in the job market can create challenges. It's important to remember that changing jobs or changing careers at any age can be time consuming.

My own example of this occurred when I was offered a position for which I interviewed. Two days following the offer of employment, it was rescinded. I was told that 'the hiring agent for my department failed to follow HR protocol'. Thus, the position needed to be re-posted and I would be notified if someone else with the same skills or additional skills would be hired instead of me. I was stunned to hear this and devastated that I may lose the opportunity!

The position was re-posted. After waiting anxiously for three weeks I was called back for an additional interview with the director of the department. During the interview, the director said, "I just wanted to meet you to see if you were looking for a position where you could coast into retirement. I'm really surprised to see how young and energetic you appear. I thought you would be really old and tired." I could have taken offense at these inappropriate and offensive statements, but I chose to be thankful for the job offer that followed.

In short, we need to be aware of people's perceptions whether they are real or imagined so we can find a way to present our talents in the best possible light.

Remember, *you* have a lot to offer! Present your resume and cover letter with careful consideration so you do not unintentionally contribute to any potential age bias. In addition, let others review it before distribution so you can be sure there are no errors.

CHAPTER 4: Rx FOR SUCCESS

Serious Self-Reflection

Prospective employers are looking to hire people with the right skills as well as the self-discipline and stamina to go the distance. To be this type of a prospective job candidate we may need to do a bit of preparation and self-reflection. This preparation and self-reflection is the action required to improve from the inside out!

Most prospective employees show up for the job interview expressing their passion about the company and the job. That's great, but passion does not guarantee commitment. Generally, but especially in highly competitive job markets, employers are more likely to hire candidates with a professional track record of action and accomplishments. It is to our advantage to prepare to demonstrate actions and accomplishments before we get to the interview.

What about the self-reflection? Why bother? The truth is that when we are holding on to deeply personal issues such as anger, jealousy, and guilt, we can be sure they will come out in the workplace (as in our personal life) in one form or another.

Of course no one is perfect. Still, if we are trying to change careers because we had difficulty getting along with other colleagues, we might need to make some changes. In short, if the problem is us changing jobs won't fix it! Therefore, it's important to take a good long look in the mirror. If something isn't quite right, it may be time to "take out the trash". Today is the right day to begin breaking any chains of bondage that are keeping us from becoming everything we are meant to be.

Shape up! Find some way to deal with the "trash". We all have experiences and difficult challenges that have had a negative residual impact on our life - this is just part of living. Still we must not be afraid of self-reflection. We should aggressively pursue serious self-reflection so we don't continue making the same mistakes or living the same old pain.

In order to mature and find inner peace, it's important to begin making the smallest improvements immediately.

We must discipline ourselves to stretch until we become fit mentally, physically, and emotionally, as an athlete would stretch his/her muscles before a strenuous activity.

It may take some time before significant improvement is noticed because some of the issues are deep within us. Still, it's important to start making even the smallest changes immediately.

Stretch until you become fit and healthy mentally, physically, and emotionally just as athlete would stretch his muscles before a strenuous activity.

After we take out the trash it's time to face our fears! Growing up, as an only child with few other children in the neighborhood to play with I would often cry, "Daddy, I am so lonely; there's nobody to play with." He always responded with the same statement, "Well, go outside and play by yourself. Just pretend you are having fun." This statement never solved my problem but it taught me that pretending is a reasonable substitute until the real thing becomes available.

Whenever we feel anxious or fearful about going to a job interview, we can still move forward in spite of the fear. Just *pretend* to be confidant until the interview is over or until you feel yourself beginning to relax. Keep in mind that the interviewer cannot see the butterflies jumping around in your stomach. Focus yourself on the skills you have to offer the prospective employer.

CHAPTER 5: MORE EDUCATION

As a graduate instructor and school administrator, I admit I am biased in favor of more education. Still, my best advice is this: don't enroll in an educational program until you carefully analyze whether or not you need it to make a career change.

When we are under stress and/or eager to achieve our career goals it's easy to make decisions that are unnecessary or unwise. Haste makes waste - as the saying goes.

Pursuit of additional education can be a good decision, but think about these questions before enrolling:

Is my skillset unrelated to the career I wish to attain? If so, you may need to consider additional education.

Do I have the time, money, and energy to meet the requirements of an educational program? Think about it. If you are struggling with work-life balance, you probably do not have time for additional education.

Additional degrees can take from 1-3 years to complete. Even convenient online education programs designed to fit personal schedules do require dedication and determination. There is more to an online class than logging in. You will definitely save time driving and sitting in class, but plan to spend a lot of time doing homework assignments. All solid academic programs are sufficiently rigorous to ensure learning.

Am I willing to take on a student loan to pay for my additional education? Remember, you must pay back the government after you are no longer enrolled in school whether you complete your degree or not. Student loans are not "free money". Know your ROI (return on investment)! Will the money you pay in tuition or student loans be earned-back when you have a new career? If so, go for it! If not, maybe additional training is a better option for you at this time.

If you do decide to pursue additional education, be sure to compare tuition and program costs of multiple accredited universities before making your final decision.

Once you begin gathering information from various institutions, you will find the enrollment counselors to be rather "pushy". Their job is to enroll students. Ignore this pressure and hype until you logic checks with your internal compass. Hold your ground until you are ready - they will wait for you.

CHAPTER 6: SKILLSET BRIDGE

Using Existing Skills to Make a Change

Often we underestimate our talents and abilities. As we mentioned previously, however, our skillset defines our marketability and determines what we have to offer a prospective employer.

Before attempting to change careers we must do a thorough self-examination of our skills. Keep in mind that some of our skills may be related to experiences in areas that were never included in our resume as full-time employment. For example, someone who painted houses over the summer while in college might have enough experience to include it in a resume for manager of a paint store.

Let's take a look at a job description then see if we can glean some critical skills the employer might be looking for when reviewing resumes.

Operations Manager - Manage, direct, and implement Operations strategies and objectives to ensure the achievement of company objectives.

Focus on management of on-time delivery of contract services while adhering to the quality requirements and production standards of company.

- Set up and/or approval of work schedules to ensure that schedules are maintained at the proper level.
- Monitor flow of materials and utilization of labor to ensure adequate production and customer service levels. Make recommendations to Executive Management when adjustments are needed.
- Review of inventories and supplies required to conduct business. Maintain efficient and cost-effective operations.
- Monitor allocation and use of personnel to ensure fulfillment of production schedules in all departments at the lowest possible cost.

- Facilitate operations and develop and/or approve project schedules of all departments.
- Assist Executive Management in conceiving, researching, planning, targeting, and controlling improve costs and maximize customer services.
- Continuously improve customer satisfaction through programs and/or training to meet customer quality and service expectations.
- Administer and manage safety and quality to provide an adequate and safe working environment.
- Facilitate assessment of and assistance in upgrading the talent base to achieve growth (i.e. reduced cost, maximize project schedule timelines and on-time customer service delivery). Suggest potential weaknesses that may require additional attention and/or training.
- Advise Executive Management and/or facilitate operations on general HR issues (i.e. potential threats and weaknesses, human capital management, employee motivation, performance tracking, monitoring employee adherence to Standard Operating Procedures (SOPs), analyzing impact of SOPs on customer service levels.).
- Other duties as assigned.

In the job description for Operations Manager, it is clear that the person applying must have solid management experience. The skillset for this position should include the following skills:

Skillset: management, customer service, basic HR, scheduling, project management, budget oversight

You might even see additional skills that would enhance a prospective employees skillset for this position, but for the purpose of this exercise we'll start with these.

Now Build *Your* Bridge

After reading the positing for Operations Manager, we can use our best judgment to extract the targeted skillset the employer is seeking. In this case the targeted skillset is:

Management, customer service, basic HR, scheduling, project management, budget oversight

Let's assume the actual skills of the person seeking this position include:

Shift management; call center representative, hiring, scheduling, budget development.

The actual skillset is very similar to the targeted skillset even though the work environments may have been quite different. In this example, a functional resume provides an opportunity for the prospective employee to briefly describe previous overlapping responsibilities. Emphasis on similarities in experiences would be highlighted in the cover letter.

CHAPTER 7: TOXIC WORKPLACE CASES

The following are true cases of real people (although the names have been changed) who struggled with employment in their own toxic work environment. These cases may provide some pieces of information that are helpful to you as you consider making your own career change.

The Case of Vivian

Avoiding employees may occur when the manager is uncertain what to do when employees display signs and symptoms of stress. Such was the case in which Vivian repeatedly commented to her supervisor that the workload was becoming unmanageable.

Others began observing her come to work early, work through lunch, and stay well into the evening day in and day out for several months. Unexpectedly, Vivian was rewarded for exceptional dedication to the company during the annual awards ceremony. Her new award further reinforced her workaholic behaviors.

Within several months of receiving her award, Vivian was promoted to another position with greater authority and additional responsibility. During her transition to the new position she was expected to complete her former responsibilities in addition to the new one. In an attempt to maintain excellence, Vivian continued her work schedule as before. In addition, however, she began taking her laptop home nightly to accommodate the extra responsibilities.

Vivian continued to articulate to her supervisor (and her supervisor's supervisor) that her workload was excessive. She openly shared her concerns that she was having difficulty staying on top of her duties. Her supervisor responded by acknowledging her feelings and assured her that "things would improve". He told Vivian that everyone was stretched to the extreme and that his workload was even more intense than hers. Beyond words, however, no actions were taken to modify the employee's workload. Vivian was left with no choice but to maintain her schedule of work just to stay afloat.

After several months, the Vivian experienced a breakdown in the office. She simply fell out of her chair onto the floor in convulsions. So as not to disrupt the work of other employees Vivian was loaded back into her office chair by the HR partner and wheeled to the front door of the company until the paramedics could arrive to transport her to the hospital.

Vivian returned to the company on a reduced work schedule against her doctor's advice. When asked to take on additional projects that would require working beyond her part-time status Vivian refused. Within approximately two months from the time of her breakdown Vivian resumed her normal work schedule. After only two weeks her job was suddenly eliminated.

Unfortunately, the company was walking the slippery slope of risk for litigation because the employee repeatedly expressed to her supervisor that the workload was becoming unmanageable. The supervisor's failure to direct Vivian to modify her work schedule along with failure to provide assistance put both the supervisor and the company at risk. It was convenient for the company to eliminate Vivian's position.

It is most regrettable that another position was not found for Vivian within the organization. Even if Vivian had been required to take a reduction in pay, the fact that she was not given this option was very telling as to the climate of the company.

The Case of Craig

The next case is an example of a toxic work environment where employee health concerns escalated out of control.

An employee named Craig experienced persistent stress on the job that, according to his physician, "contributed substantially to the onset of diabetes". Craig's health concerns were such that he was required to remain in the hospital then at home for a month.

During the month, Craig attempted to communicate with his

supervisor regarding various issues pertaining to his job. His supervisor, on the other hand, made the decision to provide no response to Craig regarding job-related issues. Instead, the supervisor directed the Craig to address all of his comments and concerns to HR.

Craig became confused and concerned about his supervisor's behavior. In an attempt to force the communication, Craig sought to receive information and feedback from his supervisor's supervisor. Craig's attempts were futile; his communication attempts were ignored.

Given that Craig was currently experiencing stress related health issues, the collective behavior from management compounded the employee's stress. After one month of medical leave Craig returned to work. He quickly found himself to be completely out of touch with current job-related issues and newly implemented procedures. Craig struggled to maintain appropriate sugar levels over the next several weeks.

In addition, Craig was faced with the stress of failing to meet his supervisor's expectations. Within a month from the time Craig returned to the office, the intentional withholding of critical job-related information by the supervisors created tremendous pressure on Craig. Finally, Craig made the decision to terminate his relationship with the employer.

Craig went home early one Friday afternoon. The next day, Craig was not schedule to work but he went back into the office. He cleaned out his desk, removed all pertinent files and information, and then never again returned. On Monday of the next week, Craig did not show up for work nor did he call to report being ill. The same thing happened on Tuesday; there was no call but Craig did not show up for work. Management had no information regarding Craig's absences leaving projects unfinished and a lot of whispers among colleagues in the office.

By Wednesday, HR distributed an interoffice memo stating that Craig has resigned. (Per company policy, two days of no call and no show indicate a voluntary resignation by the employee). By the next week, Craig's friend and colleagues reported that his "no call/no show" behavior was "in retaliation for the supervisor's lack of communication during his medical leave."

The supervisor in this situation played a part in contributing to Craig's stress and poor health early on. During Craig's medical leave the supervisor's intentional avoidance and lack of communication inflamed an already difficult situation. Periodic communication, even if it had been minimal, may have served to reduce the stress and tension between Craig and his supervisor.

In summary, avoidance of an employee is not an adequate management strategy. Conversely, some level of communication would have provided a reasonable attempt to reduce the employee's stress. The supervisor's behavior often determines the level of threat that the employee will engage in negative retaliatory behavior.

For example, prior to the employee's medical leave, if the supervisor believed that Craig was unable or unwilling to perform his duties, the proper progression of discipline and termination should have occurred. As unpleasant as it is to discipline or terminate an employee, following company policies and procedures is the professional route; it will ultimately provide protection against employee retaliation.

Stress is often the direct result of miscommunication. An infinite number of hypothetical scenarios accompanied by real or imagined threats to job security can easily consume employees when their supervisors do not clearly articulate expectations. Frequently, employees (including managers) have unspoken expectations that are not readily discernable during a job interview. In addition, changes in management may also result in a misunderstanding of unspoken expectations.

In adverse situations, management may opt for purposeful failure to communicate performance expectations; such vicious behavior that may result in physical and emotional harm to an employee. This regrettable behavior is a strategy used by some managers to build a case against an employee with the goal of termination.

Any salaried employee should have a general understanding that his/her work schedule should include more than 40 hours per week. If this schedule does not align with the employee's work-life balance goals, it's time for a change!

The Case of Alice

An unfortunate example of the unspoken expectations involved a salaried employee and co-worker named Alice. Alice was unexpectedly called into a meeting with the supervisor and HR partner to discover that the amount of time in the office was below standard. Alice expressed shock and disbelief at these comments. Upon further questioning Alice discovered that all employees in like positions were subject to the unspoken expectation of working 65 hours per week.

Alice responded to the statement of these expectations by saying that she was unaware rather than unwilling to comply. The supervisor and HR partner disagreed; they insisted that this expectation was stated during the interview process. Alice disagreed. She responded to these accusations by stating that if this expectation had been expressed during the original interview she would never have accepted the position.

Within days of this meeting Alice was given a directive to begin working 65 hours, demoted by title, removed from her office to a position on the floor, and sited for insubordination. Clearly, the decision to terminate the employee had been established in the mind of the supervisor when he articulated the previously unspoken expectation. Thus, the employee had fallen victim to the supervisor's trap with no option but to resign or be terminated.

Often, intentional pressures exerted by management may cause such stress and discomfort for the employee he/she may elect to resign. Resignation is clearly more favorable for the company because unemployment compensation is averted. In either case, management perceives this as "win".

Research reveals that the fallout from such a strategy can have both a negative and long-lasting impact on the company.

The Case of Nick and Beth

This is the story of Nick and Beth. Nick held a dotted line position to Beth's supervisor but was not directly responsible for Beth's evaluations. Nick, however, was in complete control of the professional development budget from which the funds to cover registration, travel, and meals.

There was an occasion for Beth to travel for a week of professional development training resulting in certification to enhance her job skills. Because the destination of Beth's training happened to be Nick's favorite place to go, he decided that he would accompany Beth.

It just so happened that during the week of the training Nick was also heavily involved in sale of his home; the sale was not going smoothly as there were some issues with the home inspection. Nick attended the morning session of the first day but never again returned to the training the rest of the week. Nick's justification for his non-attendance, as stated to Beth, was that the trainers were "stupid" and that the certification was nothing more than a "scam".

During dinner together mid-way through the week, Nick confided in Beth that he had a bad experience in a previous position. Nick reported to Beth that a female employee from the previous position had accused him of sexual harassment to her supervisor that resulted in his immediate termination. He further confided in Beth that he had made a promise to himself: "Before I die I am going to *take her out*. I know where she lives and I'm going to get her. I don't want to do it now because it would hurt my family, but I'll leave myself enough time to kill her." While Beth was shocked at Nick's words she said nothing in response.

Some months passed from the time of the training when Nick again became agitated and unpredictable. Beth took notice of Nick's erratic behaviors and bursts of anger in the workplace. Concluding that Nick's behavior was becoming more unpredictable by the day, she decided to share her observations with the supervisor. At that time, Beth also shared with the supervisor Nick's statement of threat against the female in his previous position. The supervisor promptly dismissed Beth's concerns.

Within a month of Beth's conversation with her supervisor she became more and more concerned. Consequently, Beth shared her concerns with a colleague. The colleague noted that he too had observed the unpredictable and erratic behaviors. The colleague also confided that he had personally witnessed a severe explosion of Nick's anger toward himself and others during a meeting while in the presence of Beth's supervisor. Unfortunately, the colleague reported to Beth that the supervisor "did nothing" to help bring Nick under control.

In this case, the manager's avoidance of Nick's violent outbursts further empowered Nick to behave in a grossly inappropriate manner in the workplace. To the dismay of the other employees who were trying to remain professional, Nick was permitted to behavior without restraint in any way he saw fit. Like an uncontrollable and vicious dog, other employees were being mangled while the supervisor looked on. Consequently, Beth's supervisor lost all respect from his employees due to his persistent lack of action.

Why some managers elect to do nothing and to avoid the obvious in some very inappropriate situations can be perplexing. In a court of law, the supervisor's willful negligence to address Nick's problems would most likely result in a "win" for the prosecution.

Nevertheless, there are some highly capable managers who choose to do nothing rather than create any "waves" that might threaten the stability of their own position. In the case of Beth, it is clear that the supervisor perceived Nick to be in a position of power with the potential to threaten his position. As a result, the supervisor opted to ignore Nick's behavior as if it simply did not exist.

Some time later, Beth became aware that her supervisor breached her confidence and informed Nick that she had shared concerns. Upon hearing this, Nick began to engage in subtle and purposeful passive aggressive actions. Suddenly, Beth was denied opportunities to attend training, cut off from critical job-related information, given time-consuming but meaningless assignments, and excluded from friendly conversations. Beth was eventually targeted for the inevitable - termination. Beth's awareness of her workplace culture would ultimately determine her future so long as she was willing to accept the harsh reality of her circumstance.

The psychopathic executive behaves in patterns much like those of an abuser. There are periods of kindness and encouragement followed by swift blows of anger and abusive treatment. The psychopath may say to the entire department, "You're playing a critical role in the company's success therefore I am counting on you all to do your part. The company depends on you to give your best. We are on the edge of greatness and it is because of your collective efforts that we will reach our goals." Then, after a brief period of time, a couple of individuals are terminated due to "right-sizing". While this is happening, the quotas and benchmarks for success are increased in quantum increments that are impossible for the employees to reach.

Such cyclical and bizarre behaviors exhibited by the executive cause employees to believe that their perceptions of the situation must be out of alignment; they question their own judgment, and sometimes their sanity, regarding their work environment. Just when the employee has reached the targeted mark, he/she finds that the mark has moved – and continues to move. The goal of the psychopath executive is to keep employees off balance and unsettled; this behavior sets the stage for the psychopath to control any situation in a multitude of ways.

Consequently, it is necessary for employees in this situation to take a periodic check of reality and organizational culture. They should continue to trust their deep inner voice. They must align their behaviors to their inner compass where the anchor of reality is fixed. In addition, they should look around for other work environments that are relatively "normal" so they do not lose sight of how a healthy company functions. Finally, they should take stock of their own willingness to continue to participate in this sick, dysfunctional game.

Summary

Every individual must make a personal decision whether to leave a toxic work environment or stay - at least until there is a clear and reasonable option. Sometimes with a lot of extra effort and political savvy an employee can "hang in there" just a bit longer. To make the best decision, however, let your inner compass assist you in determining your tolerance of a toxic work environment. No matter who you are, remain focused and never give up!

If and when you believe it's time to *GO,* be ready!

About the Author

Dr. Mary Jordan has served as a teacher and administrator in proprietary, public, and non-profit educational environments. She is a member of the Gold Key International Honour Society and faculty of a major university. She has consulted with thousands of employees and job seekers offering expertise as a coach and performance evaluator.

www.ingramcontent.com/pod-product-compliance
Lightning Source LLC
Chambersburg PA
CBHW070922180526
45168CB00005B/2118